Lexcel Client Care Toolkit

SECOND EDITION

Related titles from Law Society Publishing:

Lexcel Business Continuity Planning Toolkit
The Law Society

Lexcel Financial Management and Business Planning Toolkit
The Law Society

Lexcel Information Management Toolkit
The Law Society

Lexcel People Management Toolkit
The Law Society

Lexcel Risk Management Toolkit
The Law Society

All books from Law Society Publishing can be ordered through good bookshops or direct from our distributors, Prolog, by telephone 0870 850 1422 or email **lawsociety@prolog.uk.com**. Please confirm the price before ordering.

For further information or a catalogue, please contact our editorial and marketing office by email **publishing@lawsociety.org.uk**.

Lexcel Client Care Toolkit

SECOND EDITION

The Law Society

The Law Society

© The Law Society 2011

ISBN 978-1-907698-10-1

First edition published in 2010
This second edition published in 2011 by the Law Society
113 Chancery Lane, London WC2A 1PL

Typeset by Columns Design Ltd, Reading
Printed by Hobbs the Printers Ltd, Totton, Hants

The paper used for the text pages of this book is FSC® certified. FSC (the Forest Stewardship Council®) is an international network to promote responsible management of the world's forests.

Contents

Preface

Success in client care is fundamental to the success of a legal practice. Managing clients effectively is a field that many practices find particularly challenging. The reasons for this are as varied as the demands of individual clients themselves; however, it is generally accepted that an environment of increasing regulation, increasing competition, tight timescales and higher client expectations makes effective client care more important than ever. Effective client care is therefore a core element of the Lexcel practice management standard.

In response to growing demand from law firms, large and small, for practical assistance in this area, the Law Society has developed the *Lexcel Client Care Toolkit*.

The *Lexcel Client Care Toolkit* (second edition) is practical as opposed to theoretical in nature and aimed at assisting solicitors with their day-to-day work. It contains a range of policies, pro-formas, procedures and template letters. As such, the documents contained in the Toolkit should be amended to suit particular practice needs. These templates are also provided on a CD-Rom for ease of use.

The contents are comprehensive and include:

1. A **quality policy** – a requirement for Lexcel which sends a clear message to clients that the practice is committed to delivering excellent service at all times. Many local authorities and corporate bodies now only consider appointing firms that have a recognised quality standard in place.
2. A **client care policy** – a Lexcel requirement is that practices should have a policy that clearly describes how they work with their clients.
3. An **equality and diversity policy** – a Lexcel and Solicitors' Code of Conduct 2007 requirement. Such a policy should highlight the importance of non-discrimination and equality of opportunity, not only in the workplace but also in the provision of services to clients. An equality and diversity policy is considered essential for practices that wish to tender for work with a public body, as all public bodies have a duty to promote equality in all aspects of their working operations. Such a policy will go some way to evidencing this.
4. An **equal opportunities monitoring form** – a Lexcel requirement and essential for maintaining the diversity of your workforce. Taken further, monitoring of redundancies, disciplinary action, grievances, etc. will indicate any potential disciplinary trends occurring in an organisation.
5. An **internal complaints handling procedure** – a Lexcel and Code of Conduct requirement which enables a practice to deal effectively and efficiently with any complaints that arise. In the event of failure to resolve complaints through the internal procedure, the Legal Ombudsman requires evidence that practices have given due thought and consideration to their internal complaints handling procedure.

6. **Client care letters** – sample client care letters for use in a range of situations, such as probate, conveyancing and litigation. Used as templates, the aim is to assist a practice in structuring letters and will ensure that practices do not omit important elements of client care letters as required by the Code of Conduct.

The Toolkit has been revised to cover changes to the legal profession. In particular, the second edition includes the requirements and processes related to the new Legal Ombudsman (launched in October 2010). No reference is made to the forthcoming move to outcomes-focused regulation as confirmation of fulfilment was not known at the time of writing. Information will become available on the Solicitors Regulation Authority website in due course (**www.sra.org.uk**).

We hope that you will find the *Lexcel Client Care Toolkit* useful both as a reference guide and as a practical resource in your day-to-day work.

The Lexcel Office would like to thank Heather Stewart for her contribution to the creation of the Toolkit. We are also grateful for the support and efforts of colleagues within the Law Society who helped to produce this second edition.

Lexcel Office
The Law Society

1 Client care policy

> **Note:** Practices should note that the Client Care Manager should be someone with appropriate seniority to take on such a role.

The person with overall responsibility for the client care policy is [*name and job title*].

[*Name of practice*] is committed to delivering excellent client service and client care. Our client care policy describes what this commitment means in practice and what our clients can expect from us. We will endeavour to adhere to the principle of putting our clients first, thereby ensuring that service excellence is an integral part of the planning and delivery of all services to our clients.

In order to achieve client service excellence, [*name of practice*] aims at all times to:

- provide clients with a high quality, professional and consistent service;
- act in accordance with the Solicitors' Code of Conduct 2007 and other relevant regulatory requirements;
- act in a respectful and courteous manner in all dealings with clients;
- represent our clients' best interest;
- ensure all our staff fully understand and are committed to client care in all their interactions with clients;
- ensure we communicate effectively with our clients and with an agreed mode of communication upon request; and
- give clear legal advice.

At [*name of practice*], we make sure that our clients receive a client care letter that fully explains the level of service they will receive. In addition, we will name the person responsible for individual matters, their position in the practice and their qualifications. The client care letter will give the name of the supervisor responsible for each matter, and the name of the person who is responsible for dealing with any complaints.

In order that we can continually improve our service, we actively encourage and value feedback from our clients. We will use various methods to elicit feedback, including client satisfaction surveys and post-matter questionnaires. In addition, we monitor and evaluate client complaints to identify and address shortcomings and failings in our standard of service. Such feedback is essential to help continually gauge client perceptions of our service.

[*Name of practice*] has the above measures in place to ensure we achieve our goal of providing a quality service.

This policy will be reviewed annually on [*date*] by [*name of member in senior management team*] as part of the annual review of client care and as part of the annual review of risk, both of which are in line with Lexcel requirements.

2 Quality policy

> **Note:** Practices should note that the Quality Manager should be someone with appropriate seniority to take on such a role.

The person with overall responsibility for the quality policy is [*name and job title*].

[*Name of practice*] is committed to providing a consistently high quality service to all our clients. We are dedicated to establishing a climate where our practice continually meets, if not exceeds, client expectations and needs. It is our aim to operate and maintain a quality management system which will improve client service excellence.

Since [*date of Lexcel award*], our quality management systems have undergone an independent and rigorous annual assessment against the Lexcel practice management standard. The Lexcel standard requires that our files are subject to regular internal and external file audits. Such scrutiny ensures that any corrective action required is implemented swiftly and preventative measures are applied, where appropriate. Data and trends resulting from audits will be reviewed regularly and included in our annual review of risk.

We also hold [*insert other quality standards, e.g.* Investors in People/ISO 9001:2000], since [*date(s) of award)*].

At [*name of practice*], we aim to develop and maintain an organisational culture that encourages continuous improvement and where all levels of staff are supported and empowered. We exercise this responsibility through the continuing development of staff competency. [*Name of practice*] recognises that our employees are our greatest asset and we invest in our staff by providing regular and relevant training. Appropriately trained staff will enable us to improve the quality of service to our clients.

All our employees understand the value of their input into maintaining Lexcel [*and other quality standards, where applicable*]. We operate various systems in which staff can suggest improvements to the quality policy. For example, we maintain an online suggestion box in which staff can offer ideas for improvements. We also regularly undertake staff surveys. [*Insert other methods.*] All information submitted will be appraised and considered during the annual management review of the policy.

[*Name of practice*] has the above measures in place to ensure that we achieve our goal of providing a quality service.

This policy will be reviewed annually on [*date*] by [*name of relevant member in senior management team*] as part of an annual review of the quality management system and in line with Lexcel requirements.

3 Equality and diversity policy

Notes: Practices should note that the Equality Manager should be someone with appropriate seniority to take on such a role.

Please also see Appendix B for details of how to obtain the Law Society's *Equality and Diversity Standards and Toolkit* and Diversity and Inclusion Charter.

(Policy issued under rule 6 of the Solicitors' Code of Conduct 2007)

1 The firm's commitment

1.1 General commitment

This firm is committed to eliminating discrimination and promoting equality and diversity in its own policies, practices, procedures and work with clients and to contributing to the development of equality and diversity within the legal sector where it has the ability to do so.

This applies to the firm's professional dealings with staff and [partners]/[members]/ [directors], other solicitors, barristers, clients and third parties.

The firm intends to treat everyone equally and with dignity, courtesy and respect regardless of their disability, gender, age, race, racial group, colour, ethnic or national origin, nationality, religion or belief, sexual orientation, HIV status, trade union status, marriage or civil partnership status, spent convictions or any other personal characteristic.

1.2 Regulation and legislation

In developing and implementing its equality and diversity policy, the firm is committed to complying with rule 6 of the Solicitors' Code of Conduct 2007 and with all current and any future anti-discrimination legislation and associated codes of practice including, but not limited to:

- Equality Act 2010;
- the following codes of practice:

    (a) the Commission for Racial Equality code of practice for the elimination of racial discrimination and the promotion of equality of opportunity in employment (1983);

    (b) the Equal Opportunities Commission code of practice on sex discrimination; equal opportunities policies, procedures and practices in employment (1985);

(c) the Equal Opportunities Commission code of practice on Equal Pay (2003);

(d) the Disability Discrimination Act 1995 codes of practice in relation to rights of access to facilities, services and premises in employment;

(e) the European Community code of practice on the protection of the dignity of men and women at work;

and any relevant amendments to or further codes of practice.

Note: The Equality Act 2010 became law on 1 October 2010 and provides a new legislative framework to protect the rights and advance equality of opportunity for all. The Act simplifies and brings into one Act existing discrimination law, including:

- Equal Pay Act 1970;
- Sex Discrimination Act 1975;
- Race Relations Act 1976;
- Disability Discrimination Act 1995;
- Equality Act 2006, Part 2;
- Employment Equality (Religion or Belief) Regulations 2003;
- Employment Equality (Sexual Orientation) Regulations 2003;
- Employment Equality (Age) Regulations 2006; and
- Equality Act (Sexual Orientation) Regulations 2007.

Practices will need to check their compliance obligations under the new Act.

---

2 Forms of discrimination

The Equality Act 2010 defines the various kinds of discrimination with reference to the characteristics which are protected under the Act.

Whilst these types of discrimination largely replicate those found in previous legislation, there are some important changes which materially alter the scope of protection.

The following are the kinds of discrimination which are prohibited under this policy and the law.

2.1 Direct discrimination (s.13)

Direct discrimination occurs when someone is treated less favourably than another person because:

- they have a protected characteristic;
- they are thought to have a protected characteristic; or
- they associate with someone who has a protected characteristic.

Direct discrimination under the Act is defined as follows:

> A person (A) discriminates against another (B) if, because of a protected characteristic, A treats B less favourably than A treats or would treat others.

This definition of direct discrimination applies to all protected characteristics. In relation to the protected characteristic of age, direct discrimination can be justified if it is a proportionate means of achieving a legitimate aim.

Separate provisions exist in respect of discrimination against a woman on the grounds of pregnancy or maternity (ss.17 and 18).

2.2 Perception and association

The new definition of direct discrimination also covers a situation where someone is treated less favourably than another person because they are thought to have a protected characteristic (discrimination by perception) or because they associate with someone who has a protected characteristic (discrimination by association).

2.3 Dual discrimination (s.14)

There is a new category of dual discrimination, which allows claims of discrimination to be brought in relation to a combination of two protected characteristics. Dual discrimination claims can only be brought in relation to direct discrimination.

You should note that claims for dual discrimination only apply to the following protected characteristics: age; disability; gender reassignment; race; religion or belief; sex or sexual orientation.

Please note that the provisions relating to dual discrimination are not expected to come into force until 2011.

2.4 Indirect discrimination (s.19)

Indirect discrimination occurs when a policy or practice that applies to everyone particularly disadvantages people who share a protected characteristic. Indirect discrimination under the Act is defined as follows:

> A person (A) discriminates against another (B) if A applies to B a provision, criterion or practice which is discriminatory in relation to a relevant protected characteristic of B's.

Indirect discrimination can only be justified if you can show that the policy or practice is a proportionate means of achieving a legitimate aim.

Indirect discrimination had already applied to age, race, religion or belief, sex, sexual orientation and marriage and civil partnership. It has now been extended to cover disability and gender re-assignment. It does not apply to pregnancy or maternity.

2.5 Discrimination arising from disability (s.15)

This is a new provision. Under s.15 a person discriminates against a disabled person if that person treats them unfavourably because of something arising in consequence of their disability, and this treatment cannot be justified as a proportionate means of achieving a legitimate aim.

If you are acting as either an employer or service provider and did not know and could not reasonably have been expected to know of the disabled person's disability, then the unfavourable treatment will not amount to discrimination. However, you must do all you can reasonably be expected to do to find out if a person has a disability.

Unlike direct and indirect discrimination, this form of discrimination does not require the use of a comparator to establish less favourable treatment.

2.6 Duty to make adjustments (s.20)

The Act consolidates and extends existing duties upon employers and suppliers of goods and services from the Disability Discrimination Act 1995 to make reasonable adjustments for disabled persons.

The duty is three-fold:

- Where a provision, criterion or practice puts a disabled person at a substantial disadvantage in relation to a relevant matter in comparison with persons who are not disabled, the person to whom the duty applies must take reasonable steps to avoid the disadvantage.
- Where a physical feature puts a disabled person at a substantial disadvantage in comparison with persons who are not disabled, the person to whom the duty applies must take reasonable steps to avoid the disadvantage.
- Where a disabled person would, but for the provision of an auxiliary aid, be at a substantial disadvantage in comparison with persons who are not disabled, the person to whom the duty applies must take reasonable steps to provide the auxiliary aid.

In relation to requirements where the provision, criterion or practice in question or the auxiliary aid required relates to the provision of information, 'reasonable steps' include making sure that the information is in an accessible format. The duty referring to the provision of auxiliary aids only previously applied to premises and goods and services, but has now been extended to employment. More details about how the duty operates in the goods and services and employment contexts can be found in Schedules 2 and 8 of the Act.

2.7 Harassment

Harassment is defined in the Act as: 'unwanted conduct related to a relevant protected characteristic', which has the purpose or effect of violating an individual's dignity or 'creating an intimidating, hostile, degrading, humiliating or offensive environment' for that individual.

Harassment applies to all protected characteristics except for pregnancy and maternity, and marriage and civil partnership.

The Act specifically prohibits three types of harassment:

- harassment related to a 'relevant protected characteristic';
- sexual harassment; and
- less favourable treatment of a service user because they submit to or reject sexual harassment related to sex or gender reassignment.

For harassment related to a protected characteristic, 'related to' includes where the employee or client being harassed has a protected characteristic or where there is any connection with a protected characteristic. 'Any connection' includes a situation where the employee or client being harassed has an association with someone who has a protected characteristic or where they are perceived wrongly as having a particular protected characteristic.

You may now also be found liable for harassment by third parties who are not your employees (e.g. clients or contractors). This has been extended to cover age, disability, gender reassignment, race, religion or belief and sexual orientation.

The following must be shown for liability to be established:

- the prohibited conduct has occurred with your knowledge on at least two occasions; and
- you have not taken reasonable steps to prevent it.

A statutory defence is available to employers and principals (as service providers) who can avoid liability for harassment carried out by their employees or agents if they take all reasonable steps to prevent harassment occurring.

2.8 Victimisation (s.27)

Victimisation occurs when an employer or service provider subjects a person to a detriment because the person has carried out (or you believe they have or may carry out) what is referred to as a 'protected act'.

A protected act is any of the following (s.27(2)):

- bringing proceedings under the Act;
- giving evidence or information in proceedings brought under the Act;
- doing anything which is related to the provisions of the Act;
- making an allegation that another person has done something in breach of the Act.

The term 'detriment' has not been defined under the Act but it can be reasonably inferred that if an action has the effect of putting a person at a disadvantage or if it makes their position worse, such treatment will amount to a detriment.

The victim need not have a protected characteristic in order to be protected from victimisation under the Act; for example they could have been supporting a person with a protected characteristic who is making a claim. Claims for victimisation can only be brought by individuals and not groups.

In line with rule 6 of the Solicitors' Code of Conduct 2007, the firm will not discriminate, nor victimise or harass, in the course of its professional dealings, groups of people on the grounds set out in **1.1** above; and will make reasonable adjustments to prevent those of the firm's employees or clients who are disabled from being substantially disadvantaged.

3   Employment and training

3.1 General statement

As an employer, the firm will treat all employees and job applicants equally and fairly and not discriminate unjustifiably against them. This will, for example, include arrangements for recruitment and selection, terms and conditions of employment, access to training opportunities, access to opportunities for promotion and/or transfers, grievance and disciplinary processes, demotions, selection for redundancies, dress code, references, bonus schemes, work allocation and any other employment-related activities.

3.2 Recruitment and selection

This firm recognises the benefits of having a diverse workforce and will take steps to ensure that:

(a) it endeavours to recruit from the widest pool of qualified candidates possible;
(b) employment opportunities are open and accessible to all on the basis of candidates' individual qualities and personal merits;
(c) where appropriate, positive action measures are taken to attract applications from all sections of society and especially from those groups which are under-represented in the workforce;
(d) selection criteria and processes do not discriminate unjustifiably on the grounds of age, disability, gender reassignment, marriage or civil partnership status, race, racial group, colour, ethnic or national origin, nationality, religion or belief, sex or sexual orientation, other than in those instances where the firm is exercising permitted positive action;
(e) wherever appropriate and necessary, lawful exemptions (genuine occupational requirements) will be used to recruit suitable staff to meet the particular requirements of particular groups;
(f) all recruitment agencies acting for the firm are required to be aware of this policy and its requirement not to discriminate and to act in accordance with this policy and the law.

3.3 Conditions of service

The firm will treat all employees equally and strive to create a working environment which is free from discrimination and harassment and which respects, where appropriate, the diverse backgrounds and beliefs of employees.

Terms and conditions of service for employees will comply with anti-discrimination legislation. The provision of benefits such as working hours, maternity and other leave arrangements, performance appraisal systems, dress code, bonus schemes and any other conditions of employment, will not discriminate against any employee on the grounds of his or her gender, marital status, race, racial group, colour, ethnic or national origin, nationality, religion or belief, or sexual orientation; or unreasonably on the grounds of his or her disability.

The firm will endeavour to provide appropriate facilities and conditions of service which take into account the specific needs of employees which arise from their ethnic or cultural background, gender, responsibilities as carers, disability, religion or belief, or sexual orientation.

3.4 Promotion and career development

Promotion within the firm (including to [partners]/[members]/[directors]) will be made without reference to any of the forbidden grounds and will be based solely on merit.

The selection criteria and processes for recruitment and promotion will be kept under review to ensure that there is no unjustifiably discriminatory impact on any particular group.

Whilst positive action measures may be taken in accordance with the relevant anti-discrimination legislation to encourage under-represented groups to apply for promotion opportunities, recruitment or promotion to all jobs will be based solely on merit.

All employees will have access to appropriate training and other career development opportunities. However, the firm will take appropriate positive action measures (as permitted by the anti-discrimination legislation) to provide additional support, encouragement to apply and relevant guidance for groups which are under-represented in the workforce and ensure that access to development opportunities are made on an equal and fair basis.

4   [Partners]/[Members]/[Directors]

Arrangements and procedures for selecting [partners]/[members]/[directors], their terms and conditions of [partnership]/[membership]/[directorship], access to benefits, facilities or services and termination arrangements will be reviewed and amended where necessary to prevent discrimination on any of the forbidden grounds.

Maternity rights available to [partners]/[members]/[directors] shall be no less favourable that those required by legislation for employees.

5 Barristers and third parties

5.1 Barristers

Barristers should be instructed on the basis of their skills, experience and ability. The firm will not, on any of the forbidden grounds, avoid briefing a barrister and will not request barristers' clerks to do so.

Clients' requests for a named barrister should be complied with, subject to the firm's duty to discuss with the client the suitability of the barrister and to advise appropriately.

The firm will discuss with the client any request by the client that only a barrister who is not disabled or who is of a particular gender, marital status, race, racial group, colour, ethnic or national origin, nationality, religion or belief, or sexual orientation, be instructed. In the absence of a valid reason for this request, which must be within the exemptions permitted by the anti-discrimination legislation, the firm will endeavour to persuade the client to modify their instructions in so far as they are given on discriminatory grounds. Should the client refuse to modify such instructions, the firm will cease to act, as carrying out instructions to discriminate is unlawful and the firm would be liable for any such action.

5.2 Suppliers

All lists of approved suppliers and databases of contractors, agents and other third parties who, or which, are regarded as suitable to be instructed by those within the firm, have been compiled only on the basis of the ability of those persons or organisations to undertake work of a particular type and contain no discriminatory exclusion, restriction or preference. Reasonable measures are in place to ensure that sound equality and diversity policies are in place with those from whom the firm purchases goods and services.

6 Clients

The firm is generally free to decide whether to accept instructions from any particular client, but any refusal to act will not be based upon any of the forbidden grounds.

The firm will take steps to meet the different needs of particular clients arising from its obligations under the anti-discrimination legislation (such as the Equality Act 2010 and clauses relating to disability discrimination) and rule 6 of the Solicitors' Code of Conduct 2007.

In addition, where necessary and where it is permitted by the relevant anti-discrimination legislation (for example, provisions relating to positive action or exemptions), the firm will seek to provide services which meet the specific needs and requests arising from clients' ethnic or cultural background, gender, responsibilities as carers, disability, religion or belief, sexual orientation or other relevant factors.

7   Promoting equality and diversity

This firm is committed to promoting equality and diversity in the firm as well as in those areas in which it has influence [and is signed up to the Law Society's Equality and Inclusion Charter and the use of the supporting best practice protocols].

Employees and [partners]/[members]/[directors] will be informed of this equality and diversity policy and will be provided with equality and diversity training appropriate to their needs and responsibilities.

All those who act on the firm's behalf will be informed of this equality and diversity policy and will be expected to pay due regard to it when conducting business on the firm's behalf.

In all its dealings, including those with suppliers, contractors and recruitment agencies and any other third parties, the firm will seek to promote the principles of equality and diversity and will take reasonable steps to ensure appropriate standards in relation to this policy are maintained. The firm will make every effort to reflect its commitment to equality and diversity in its marketing and communication activities including, but not limited to, accessible print and online formats.

8   Implementing the policy

8.1 Responsibility

Ultimate responsibility for implementing the policy rests with the [principal]/ [partners]/[members]/[directors] of the firm. The firm will appoint a senior person within it to be responsible for the operation of the policy.

All employees and [partners]/[members]/[directors] of the firm are expected to pay due regard to the provisions of its equality and diversity policy and are responsible for ensuring compliance with it when undertaking their jobs or representing the firm.

Acts of discrimination or harassment on any of the forbidden grounds by employees or [partners]/[members]/[directors] of the firm will result in disciplinary action. Failure to comply with this policy will be treated in a similar fashion. The policy applies to all who are employed in the firm, whether full-time, part-time, temporary or agency staff, and to all [partners]/[members]/[directors].

Acts of discrimination or harassment on any of the forbidden grounds by those acting on behalf of the firm will lead to appropriate action which may include termination of services.

8.2 Complaints of discrimination

The firm will treat seriously, and will take appropriate action concerning, all complaints of discrimination or harassment on any of the forbidden grounds made by employees, [partners]/[members]/[directors], clients, barristers or other third parties.

All complaints will be investigated in accordance with the firm's discipline and grievance and/or complaints procedure and the complainant will be informed of the outcome.

8.3 Monitoring and review

The policy will be monitored and reviewed in a manner proportionate to the size and nature of the firm on a regular basis (and in any event at least annually) to measure its progress and judge the effectiveness of the policy provisions. Monitoring information will always be used anonymously as statistical trends and managed in accordance with the Data Protection Act 1998, and treated with the highest level of confidentiality.

In particular, the firm will, as appropriate, monitor and record:

(a) the age, sexual orientation, gender, and ethnic composition of the workforce and partners as well as the number of disabled staff, [partners]/[members]/[directors] at different levels of the organisation;

(b) the age, sexual orientation, ethnicity, gender and disability of all applicants, short-listed applicants and successful applicants for jobs and training contracts;

(c) the ethnicity, gender and disability of all applicants for promotion (including to partnership, to the role of a member of a limited liability partnership or as director of a recognised body) and training opportunities and details of whether they were successful;

(d) the sexual orientation and religion or belief of all [partners]/[members]/[directors] and staff so as to ensure that they are not being discriminated against in terms of the opportunities or benefits available to them. Firms should, however, be aware that [partners]/[members]/[directors] and staff may choose not to disclose their individual data and they are within their rights to refuse to provide this information;

(e) the number and outcome of complaints of discrimination made by staff, [partners]/[members]/[directors], barristers, clients and other third parties;

(f) the disciplinary action (if any) taken against employees by race, gender and disability.

This information will be used to review the progress and impact of the equality and diversity policy and related practices. Any changes required will be made and implemented within a reasonable timeframe.

4 Equality and diversity statement

(a) [*Name of practice*] is fully committed to equality and diversity in all of its functions. [*Name of practice*] believes that everyone has a right to be treated with dignity and respect and seeks to ensure that the principles of fairness and equality of opportunity for all underpin all its policies, plans, procedures, processes and practices. Please contact us if you would like a copy of our equality and diversity policy via: [*insert contact details*].

OR

(b) [*Name of practice*] is committed to promoting equality and diversity in all its dealings with clients, third parties and employees. Please contact us if you would like a copy of our equality and diversity policy via: [*insert contact details*].

OR

(c) [*Name of practice*] aims to be an inclusive employer and will select staff solely on merit, irrespective of race, sex, disability, age, religion or belief, or sexual orientation. In order to monitor the effectiveness of our equality and diversity policy, we request all applicants to provide us the information asked for on the job application form. A copy of the policy is available on request via: [*insert contact details*].

OR

(d) [*Name of practice*] aims to promote equality of opportunity in employment, in its dealing with clients and in service delivery, and has a policy for this purpose. The policy covers all aspects of employment, from advertising vacancies, recruitment and selection, training and conditions of service, and all aspects of professional dealings with clients, including the engagement of professional services. A copy of the policy is available on request via: [*insert contact details*].

5 Equality and diversity monitoring form

[*Name of practice*] operates an equality and diversity policy. To help us monitor its effectiveness, please complete this monitoring form. All responses will be kept confidential.

Gender

What is your gender?	Male ☐	Female ☐

Disability

Do you consider yourself as having a disability?	Yes ☐	No ☐

If yes, please give more information about your disability (delete as appropriate).

Physical ☐	Visual ☐	Hearing ☐	Mental health ☐
Learning disabilities ☐	Another illness ☐	Please specify:	

*The Equality Act 2010 defines disability as a physical or mental impairment which has a substantial and long-term effect on a person's ability to carry out normal day-to-day activities.

Ethnic origin

Please tick the box from the list below which best describes the ethnic group to which you belong:

White		Black or Black British		Chinese or other ethnic group	
British	☐	Black Caribbean	☐	Chinese	☐
Irish	☐	Black African	☐	Other ethnic background	☐
Other white background	☐	Other black background	☐	Other Asian background	☐
Please specify:		Please specify:		Please specify:	
Mixed		**Asian or Asian British**			
White & Black Caribbean	☐	Indian	☐		
White & Black African	☐	Pakistani	☐		
White & Asian	☐	Bangladeshi	☐		
Please specify:		Please specify:			

Religious beliefs

Please tick the box from the list below which best describes your religious belief:

Agnostic	☐	Atheist	☐	Christian	☐	Hindu	☐
Jewish	☐	Muslim	☐	Roman Catholic	☐	Sikh	☐
Not specified	☐	Other	☐	Please specify:		

Sexual orientation

Please tick the box from the list below which best describes your sexual orientation:

| Not specified | ☐ | Same sex (homosexual) | ☐ |
| Opposite sex (heterosexual) | ☐ | Same sex and opposite sex (bisexual) | ☐ |

Age

| 16–25 | ☐ | 41–55 | ☐ |
| 26–40 | ☐ | 55+ | ☐ |

Advertising

To help us monitor our advertising policy, please say where you saw this post advertised.

Thank you for completing this questionnaire. Please return this form to [*name*] via [*insert contact details*].

6 Complaints handling statement

(a) [*Name of practice*] is committed to high quality legal advice and client care. If you are unhappy about any aspect of the service you have received please contact [*name*] on [*phone number and email*] or by post to our office at [*postal address*]. A copy of our complaints policy is available on request via: [*insert contact details*].

OR

(b) We at [*name of practice*] are committed to providing a high quality legal service to all our clients. If you are unhappy with any aspects of our service we want to know about it as we take all complaints seriously. If you have a complaint, please contact [*name*] on [*phone number and email*] or by post to our office at [*postal address*]. A copy of our complaints policy is available on request via: [*insert contact details*].

7 Complaints handling procedure

> **Note:** From 6 October 2010 the Legal Ombudsman replaced the Legal Complaints Service which previously dealt with consumer complaints. There are some significant differences between the two schemes and practices should familiarise themselves with the Legal Ombudsman's Scheme Rules to ensure they provide clients with accurate and appropriate information.

Our complaints handling policy

[*Name of practice*] is committed to providing a high quality legal service to all our clients. When something goes wrong, we need you to tell us about it. This will help us to improve our standards.

Our complaints handling procedure

If you have a concern or a complaint, please contact us as soon as you are aware of the problem so this can be addressed. [*Insert contact details.*]

> **Note:** Firms may wish to provide clients with a copy of the 'Making a complaint' leaflet which is produced by the Legal Ombudsman (**www.legalombudsman. org.uk/aboutus/publications.html**).

What will happen next?

1. We will send you a letter acknowledging receipt of your complaint within five days of your raising your concerns, enclosing a copy of this procedure. [*Consider format for those who are vulnerable or have disabilities.*]
2. We will then investigate your complaint. This will normally involve passing your complaint to our client care partner, [*name*], who will review your matter file and speak to the member of staff who acted for you.
3. [*Name*] will then invite you to a meeting to discuss and, it is hoped, resolve your complaint. S/he will do this within 14 days of sending you the acknowledgement letter.
4. Within three days of the meeting, [*name*] will write to you to confirm what took place and any solutions s/he has agreed with you.

5. If you do not want a meeting or it is not possible, [*name*] will send you a detailed written reply to your complaint, including his/her suggestions for resolving the matter, within 21 days of sending you the acknowledgement letter.

6. At this stage, if you are still not satisfied, you should contact us again to explain why you remain unhappy with our response and we will review your comments. Depending on the matter we may at this stage arrange for another partner to review the decision.

7. We will write to you within 14 days of receiving your request for a review, confirming our final position on your complaint and explaining our reasons.

8. If you are still not satisfied, you can then contact the Legal Ombudsman at PO Box 15870, Birmingham B30 9EB or call 0300 555 0333 about your complaint. Any complaint to the Legal Ombudsman must usually be made within six months of your receiving a final written response from us regarding your complaint. The Legal Ombudsman has provided further guidance on its service at **www.legalombudsman.org.uk**.

If we have to change any of the timescales above, we will let you know and explain why.

8 Complaints management checklist

The checklist below is a useful reminder for the complaints handling partner and/or fee earner.

	Completed	Date completed	Next action date
Start new internal complaint form	☐		
Acknowledge complaint within 5 days	☐		
Advise client who is considering their complaint	☐		
Give client a timeframe for a response	☐		
Client's communication preferences received	☐		
Provide internal complaints procedure and information on Legal Ombudsman	☐		
Identify and clarify all complaints raised	☐		
Consider from client's point of view	☐		
Advise fee earner	☐		
Respond in 21 days	☐		
Explain steps taken to investigate	☐		
Demonstrate client's concerns have been considered	☐		
Explain reasons for views held in respect of each complaint	☐		
Apologise/offer remedy where appropriate	☐		
Remind of option to go to Legal Ombudsman and provide its contact details and time limits for complaints acceptance	☐		

9 Complaint register

Date complaint received			
Name of client			
Fee earner involved			
Fee earner's supervisor			
Nature of complaint			
Date of start of investigation		Date of letter to client explaining process	
Location of letter on IT system			
Date of any internal meeting with client			
Outcome of investigation			
Date of letter to client at end of investigation			
Location of letter on IT system			
Is the complaint resolved?	Yes ☐	No ☐	
Referral to Legal Ombudsman	Yes ☐	No ☐	
Brief overview of complaint			

10 Client complaint form

> **Note:** Practices should make provisions for complaints to be made by any reasonable means. The form below is a useful way of capturing key information but should be optional for clients to complete.

[*Name of practice*] is eager to resolve complaints made by its clients. To help us understand and examine your complaint, please complete the form below. We aim to respond to your initial complaint within [*state duration*].

Client contact details

Title	Mr ☐ Mrs ☐ Ms ☐ Miss ☐ Other ☐		Please specify:
Surname		First name(s)	
Address including postcode			
Daytime telephone		Mobile telephone	
Email			

Information for the complaints handling partner

Name of solicitor	
Solicitor or case reference	

Detail of the complaint

Nature or detail of complaint (please give dates and examples if possible)	

Please select as appropriate	I am happy for you to deal with my complaint in writing	☐
	I would prefer you to arrange a meeting to discuss my complaint	☐
	I would like you to do the following to sort out my complaint	☐
	Please state:	
Your signature		Date

If you get a reply which you are not happy with, please call the Legal Ombudsman helpline on 0300 555 0333.

11 Client care letter – conveyancing

[Law firm contact details]

[Client's/clients' name]

[Client's/clients' address]

[Date]

Our ref: *[practice ref]*

Your ref: *[client ref]*

Dear *[client's name – insert all if more than one purchaser]*

Your purchase of [address of property]

Thank you for asking this firm to act for you in connection with your proposed purchase of *[address of property]*. This letter, and the accompanying terms and conditions of business, set out the basis under which *[practice name]* will carry out the work on your behalf.

Your instructions

You want to buy *[address]* for the agreed price of £*[amount]*, subject to contract, with the help of a loan from *[lender's name]*, and you have agreed that we shall also be advising *[lender's name]* in relation to the purchase.

Responsibility for your matter

My name is *[name]* and I am *[precise status]*. I shall be carrying out the work relating to your purchase. [[*Supervisor's name*] is the *[specify supervisor's role]* and is ultimately responsible for your matter and supervises this *[department/team]*].

I can usually be contacted by telephone on [*number*] between [9.30 am and 5.30 pm] on weekdays. [*Name*] who is a [paralegal]/[assistant] will be able to help you with any queries if I am not available when you call.

Costs and expenses

We have agreed a fixed fee of £[*amount*] with you for completing your purchase. The work will consist of the following:

(a) investigating the title to the property, to include:

    (i)   carrying out searches with respect to title and local government information for the property;

    (ii) reviewing replies given by the seller to pre-contract enquiries;

(b) negotiating a purchase contract;

(c) negotiating a transfer document;

(d) advising you in respect of your mortgage offer;

(e) preparing a report on title;

(f) proceeding to exchange of contracts and then completion of the purchase;

(g) transferring funds by telegraphic transfer to the seller's solicitors and for relevant taxes;

(h) calculating stamp duty land tax (SDLT) on the purchase and preparing and submitting to HM Revenue and Customs the appropriate SDLT forms; and

(i) registering the purchase and the mortgage at the Land Registry.

Our fees are:

Fixed purchase price	£
VAT	£
Telegraphic transfer fee	£
VAT	£
[*Practice name*] total fees	£

[The price has been calculated on the basis that [*specify assumptions, e.g.*]:

(a) the property is currently held under a single freehold title at the Land Registry with no title defects;

(b) one contract is submitted to one purchaser;

(c) the purchase will be on the basis of an unconditional contract and the property is acquired with vacant possession;

(d) completion takes place on the date agreed in the contract;

(e) [*any other assumptions or exclusions*].]

If it becomes apparent that there are unforeseen circumstances in connection with the purchase we may have to increase our charges but, if that is the case, I shall inform you before we incur any additional costs.

In addition, there are a number of expenses which have to be paid to third parties to enable us to complete your purchase. These charges must also be paid by you.

The other likely expenses are:

Search fees (estimate)	£
Land Registry fee	£
Stamp duty land tax	£
Total expenses	£

If we find that any additional expenses need to be incurred after we have considered the contract, searches and title documents, I shall let you know the reason for the extra expense, the likely amount, and when I shall need payment.

If, for any reason, we have to abort the transaction related to the purchase of your property, I will break the transaction down into stages and advise what percentage of the estimated fee will be charged at each stage.

When you need to pay

We shall have to pay the search fees listed above very shortly. Please therefore let me have a cheque for £[amount] made out to [practice name] to cover the cost of these as soon as possible to avoid any delay as I cannot send the searches until I receive this amount from you.

I shall send you a statement showing all the other amounts due, including our fees, shortly before completion.

Next steps

I have asked the seller's solicitors to let me have a draft contract and other papers relating to the title to the property. As soon as I receive these, I shall begin the requisite searches in respect of the property which I estimate will take [timeframe]. I shall write to you as soon as I have all the information, including your mortgage offer, and we can arrange a convenient appointment for you to call to discuss the contract and searches.

If everything is in order, we shall then be in a position to exchange contracts with the seller's solicitor, after which both you and the seller will be bound to proceed to complete the sale and purchase. A non-refundable deposit of £[amount] will be payable by you on exchange of contracts and I shall ask you to let me have this amount when we are ready to exchange. The timing of the exchange will also depend on when the seller is in a position to do so. When we exchange contracts we shall agree a mutually convenient date for completion, the day on which you gain possession of the house.

The balance of the purchase price, including our fees but excluding the amount of your mortgage loan from [name of lender], will have to be paid to us a few days before the completion date to allow us to have cleared funds for the completion.

I understand that you wish to complete the purchase by [date], and while we shall do our best to achieve this, our ability to do so may be affected by matters outside our control.

Money laundering requirements

The law requires solicitors, banks, building societies and others to obtain satisfactory evidence of the identity of their client and, at times, people related to the client or their case. This is because solicitors who deal with money and property on behalf of their client can be used by criminals wanting to launder money.

In order to comply with the law on money laundering, we need to obtain evidence of your identity as soon as practicable, and in any event before we can proceed with your matter. To collect this evidence, our practice is to [insert your standard practice, e.g. take a photocopy of your original passport and a copy of a utility bill].

If you are unable to provide us with the specific identification requested, please contact our office as soon as possible so that we can discuss alternative ways to verify your identity.

Our service

[Practice name] is committed to high quality legal advice and client care. If you are unhappy about any aspect of the service you receive, or about the bill, please contact [name] on [telephone number], via email at [email address] or by post to [office name and address].

We have a procedure in place which details how we handle complaints, available at [insert details]. If you are not satisfied with our handling of your complaint you can ask the Legal Ombudsman to consider the complaint. Normally, you will need to bring a complaint to the Legal Ombudsman within six months of receiving a final written response from us about your complaint.

The Legal Ombudsman can be contacted at PO Box 15870, Birmingham B30 9EB, or by calling 0300 555 0333.

You also have the right to object to the bill and apply for an assessment of the bill under Part III of the Solicitors Act 1974. The Legal Ombudsman may not deal with a complaint about the bill if you have applied to the court for an assessment of the bill.

Terms of business

I also enclose this firm's terms and conditions of business which contain further important information about the way in which we shall carry out the work we do for you. If you have any queries or want to discuss any term further, please do not hesitate to contact me.

Your continuing instructions in this matter will be taken as acceptance of these terms of business and the information in this letter. However, I also enclose a duplicate copy of this letter and the terms of business and shall be grateful if you will sign and return both to us in the enclosed stamped addressed envelope as soon as possible so that we have a clear record of the terms of our agreement.

Yours sincerely,

[*Signatory*]

12 Client care letter – employment

[*Law firm contact details*]

[*Client's/clients' name*]

[*Client's/clients' address*]

[*Date*]

Our ref: [*practice ref*]

Your ref: [*client ref*]

Dear [*client's name*]

Tribunal claim – employee

Thank you for instructing [*name of practice*] in connection with your claim against [*name of other party*]. We confirm that we shall be pleased to act for you in the matter.

This letter, and the accompanying terms and conditions of business, set out the basis under which [*practice name*] will carry out the work on your behalf. They explain how we will manage your matter and detail the people who will be responsible for the work. They also set out how this firm's costs will be calculated. Please do read both the letter and terms of business carefully, but do not hesitate to contact me if you have any queries or would like to discuss any term further.

Responsibility for your matter

I am a [*specify precise status*] and shall have responsibility for the day-to-day conduct of your matter. Other members of the employment team who may assist me from time to time are set out [in Schedule 1 to this letter]. [[*Supervisor's name*] is the [*specify supervisor's role*] and is ultimately responsible for the matter and supervises this [department]/[team].]

I can usually be contacted by telephone on [*number*] between [9.30 am and 5.30 pm] on weekdays. [*Name*] who is a [paralegal]/[assistant] will be able to help you with any queries if I am not available when you call.

Your instructions

[Your objective in the claim is [*set out objective and name of other party*].]

Agreed next steps

[I have agreed to lodge an Employment Tribunal claim on your behalf at the [*name*] Employment Tribunal. The claims will be for: [*specify claims*].

As soon as you return the enclosed documents to me, duly signed, I shall draft an Employment Tribunal claim and send it to you for your comments. When you have approved it, I shall lodge the claim with the Tribunal.]

Timescales

Assuming that [*name of other party*] defend your claim, I anticipate that it will take between [*minimum*] and [*maximum*] months to obtain a decision from the Employment Tribunal. That timescale may be shorter if we achieve a settlement with [*name of other party*].

How can this be paid for?

[*Outline the options for third parties to pay for the matter, i.e. existing insurer, trade union, after-the-event insurance, and the steps the client needs to take to enable these options to be explored. If these have already been considered and are not available – state this.*]

[*If your firm offers contingency fee arrangements for employment work, set out the details of this option – for more information on what to say, see rules 2.03 and 2.06 of the Solicitors' Code of Conduct 2007, the Practice Advice Service booklet, 'Contentious costs', and their 'Payment by Results' booklet.*]

[*Outline private payment options in brief, including hourly rates and reference to the ability of the client to set a limit – then refer to the details in the terms and conditions.*]

Can I get an order for costs?

If you are not successful in your claim, you may have to pay [*name of other party's*] costs. For further information about court awards for costs, please see our terms of business.

What do you have to pay now?

[*Practice name*] requests that clients make a payment of £[500.00] at the beginning of any matter and I ask that you let us have a cheque for this amount as soon as possible. Alternatively, you can send this electronically to our client account at:

[*specify bank details*]

[*ensure full client reference details specified*].

Our service

[*Practice name*] is committed to high quality legal advice and client care. If you are unhappy about any aspect of the service you receive, or about the bill, please contact [*name*] on [*telephone number*], via email at [*email address*] or by post to [*office name and address*].

We have a procedure in place which details how we handle complaints, available at [*insert details*]. If you are not satisfied with our handling of your complaint you can ask the Legal Ombudsman to consider the complaint. Normally, you will need to bring a complaint to the Legal Ombudsman within six months of receiving a final written response from us about your complaint.

The Legal Ombudsman can be contacted at PO Box 15870, Birmingham B30 9EB, or by calling 0300 555 0333.

You also have the right to object to the bill and apply for an assessment of the bill under Part III of the Solicitors Act 1974. The Legal Ombudsman may not deal with a complaint about the bill if you have applied to the court for an assessment of the bill.

I have enclosed a second copy of both this letter and the terms of business of [*practice name*]. We ask that you sign them and return them to us so that we can commence acting on your behalf.

Yours sincerely

[*Signatory*]

13 Client care letter – matrimonial

> **Notes:** Please refer to the Law Society Practice Note 'Client care letters' (2010) for the content of a client care letter and for sample terms and conditions of business.
>
> This suggested client care letter is by way of example only to show that it need not be a lengthy document. Practices must not rely upon it and must draft their own letter to ensure that they comply fully with the requirements of the Solicitors' Code of Conduct 2007.

[*Law firm contact details*]

[*Client's/clients' name*]

[*Client's/clients' address*]

[*Date*]

Our ref: [*practice ref*]

Your ref: [*client ref*]

Dear [*client's name*]

Your marriage difficulties

I was pleased to meet you on [*day*] and thank you for asking this firm to act for you in obtaining a divorce and resolving the consequent financial issues.

I am writing to confirm the matters we discussed and to ensure a clear understanding about the way in which [*practice name*] will carry out the work. This letter, and the accompanying terms of business, set out the basis on which we will act for you. They explain how we will manage your matter and detail the people who will be responsible for the work. They also set out how this firm's costs are calculated and your responsibility for paying them. Please do read both the letter and the terms of business carefully and do not hesitate to contact me if you have any queries or would like to discuss any term further.

Responsibility for your matter

I am a [*specify precise status*] and I shall carry out most of the work in your matter. [*Supervisor's name*] is [*specify supervisor's status*] who supervises the family [department]/[team] and is ultimately responsible for your matter.

[*Name*] who is a [paralegal]/[assistant/secretary] will be able to help you with any queries if I am not available when you call.

Your instructions

You have instructed us to obtain a divorce as soon as possible and then to deal with maintenance for you and your children and the division of the assets owned by you and/or your husband. As I explained, the divorce itself involves the following stages:

[*outline all stages of a divorce from filing to decree absolute, or refer to any guidance leaflet from firm*].

Obtaining a divorce usually takes [*number*] weeks. We can then deal with [*outline potential issues for ancillary relief*]. Resolving these issues can take some time and it is impossible to say at this stage how long it will take. Usually, these matters take the following course:

[*brief outline of usual stages of an ancillary relief matter or refer to any guidance leaflet from firm*].

However, from what you told me, you are anxious that we reach an amicable settlement if at all possible and I shall work towards achieving this.

[Please note that my advice will not cover tax advice, although I shall be pleased to provide any information which your [*role of other adviser*] may need to advise you fully.]

Costs and expenses

Your divorce

As I explained, we are able to carry out the work in connection with the divorce itself for a fixed fee.

Fee for divorce	£
VAT	£
[*Practice name*] total fees	£

[The price has been calculated on the basis that:

[*set out assumptions or exclusions*].]

If it becomes apparent that there are unforeseen circumstances in connection with the divorce, we may have to increase our charges, but if that is the case, we shall inform you before we incur any additional costs.

In addition, there are a number of expenses which we shall have to pay to third parties. These charges must also be paid by you.

The other likely expenses are:

Court fee on filing petition	£
[VAT]	£
[*specify any other known expenses*]	
Total expenses	£

Resolving financial issues

[We discussed the possibility of you obtaining legal aid but [*give brief explanation of why option not available*].]

[*Outline private payment options in brief, including hourly rates and reference to the ability of the client to set a limit – then refer to the details in the terms and conditions – for more information on what to say, see rule 2.03 of the Solicitors' Code of Conduct 2007.*

Example: Our charges will be based on the time spent by me or my colleagues on your matter. The hourly rates for the time spent by each fee earner involved in the matter are set out in our terms and conditions of business. These may increase from time to time but we shall notify you before any work at the new rate is carried out.]

Expenses

There may also be expenses relating to this stage of your matter such as the fees of a barrister. I shall let you have details of these as soon as it becomes apparent that we need to incur any expense.

Invoices

As we discussed, we shall submit an invoice for the agreed fee for your divorce and expenses as soon as [*specify when bill to be sent*]. Invoices for subsequent work will be sent to you on a monthly basis for work we have done during that period. Although we cannot give you a figure for the total cost of this aspect of the work, we will discuss costs with you on a regular basis and at least once in every six-month period.

All our invoices are payable in accordance with our terms of business.

Money on account of costs

[*Practice name*] requests that clients make a payment of £500.00 at the beginning of any matter and I ask that you let us have a cheque for this amount as soon as possible. Alternatively, you can send this electronically to our client account at:

[*specify bank details*]

[*ensure full client reference details specified*].

The next steps

As we discussed, I shall:

[*outline agreed steps*].

To enable me to take these steps, I need the following from you as soon as possible:

[*outline requirements from client*].

Our service

[*Practice name*] is committed to high quality legal advice and client care. If you are unhappy about any aspect of the service you receive, or about the bill, please contact [*name*] on [*telephone number*], via email at [*email address*] or by post to [*office name and address*].

We have a procedure in place which details how we handle complaints, available at [*insert details*]. If you are not satisfied with our handling of your complaint you can ask the Legal Ombudsman to consider the complaint. Normally, you will need to bring a complaint to the Legal Ombudsman within six months of receiving a final written response from us about your complaint.

The Legal Ombudsman can be contacted at PO Box 15870, Birmingham B30 9EB, or by calling 0300 555 0333.

You also have the right to object to the bill and apply for an assessment of the bill under Part III of the Solicitors Act 1974. The Legal Ombudsman may not deal with a complaint about the bill if you have applied to the court for an assessment of the bill.

Yours sincerely

[*Signatory*]

14 Closing letter

[*Client's/clients' name*]

[*Client's/clients' address*]

[*Date*]

Our ref: [*practice ref*]

Your ref: [*client ref*]

Dear [*client's name – insert all if more than one client*]

[Name of matter]

As you know we have now concluded the work in relation to [*specify and, if appropriate, outline all steps that have been taken with concluding results*].

- Outline any action the client may need to take in the future with time limits if applicable.
- Return any documents/papers that you have been holding on behalf of the client.
- Specify any documents you are to keep in safe custody for the client with details of where they will be held, how long they will be held for, a reference number and details of whom they should contact for retrieval.
- Specify any charges for retrieval.
- Enclose copies of any documents that the client may need for reference purposes, e.g. completed copy wills, leases, land/charge certificates, copy of court orders.
- Specify whereabouts of any documents which the client is not to receive, e.g. charge certificate.
- Confirm that you no longer hold any monies on behalf of the client.
- Explain why you are holding any monies, and that you will issue an annual reminder.
- Account for any interest on monies held on behalf of client if appropriate.
- Enclose client feedback form if relevant with stamped addressed envelope.

It has been a pleasure to act on your behalf. I enclose a brochure about the other services that [*practice name*] offers and we look forward to being of service to you in the future.

Yours sincerely

[*Signatory*]

15 Change of matter handler letter

[*Law firm contact details*]

[*Client's/clients' name*]

[*Client's/clients' address*]

[*Date*]

Our ref: [*practice ref*]

Your ref: [*client ref*]

Dear [*client's name – insert all if more than one client*]

[Name of matter]

I am sorry to let you know that as from [*date*] I shall no longer be able to deal with this matter on your behalf because I am [*specify reason – e.g. transferring departments within the firm/leaving the firm/going on maternity leave, etc.*]. [*Name*] who is a [*specify precise status*] will have the responsibility for the day-to-day conduct of the matter from that date and [[*supervisor's name*] will continue to supervise the work] [[*new supervisor's name*] will take over the responsibility for the supervision of the file].

In all other respects, the terms upon which the work will be conducted as set out in our letter to you dated [*date of client care/terms of engagement letter*] will remain the same. [The hourly rate of [*name of new fee earner*] is the same as my own, £[*amount*].]

I shall ensure that [*name of new fee earner*] is fully briefed on the current position on your matter before I leave, and understand that [s]he will be in touch with you soon after [s]he takes over responsibility for it.

Yours sincerely

[*Signatory*]

16 Cost update letter

[Law firm contact details]

[Client's/clients' name]

[Client's/clients' address]

[Date]

Our ref: *[practice ref]*

Your ref: *[client ref]*

Dear *[client's name – insert all if more than one client]*

[Name of matter]

Further to our [telephone conversation]/[meeting] I confirm that to date, the fees incurred are £*[amount]*. This is within the original estimate we provided, which was £*[amount]*, for the reasons set out above. However, we now need to revise that estimate and consider that our revised estimate will be £*[amount]*. *[Explain the circumstances for change in the nature of the matter.]* A considerable amount of additional work may be involved in resolving this and *[practice name]* can no longer proceed on the basis of *[set out basis of original fee arrangement, e.g. fixed price/ estimate]* set out in our letter to you dated *[date of client care/terms of engagement letter]*.

Responsibility for your matter

[Name and status of anyone else to be involved in the conduct of the matter] will now handle the matter on your behalf [and I shall continue to assist].

Our revised charges

[We are prepared to undertake all the work involved in your matter at the increased fixed price of £*[amount]* plus VAT.

Increased price	£
VAT	£
[Practice name] total fees	£

This figure is in substitution for the figure of £[*old price including VAT*] which we gave to you in our letter dated [*date of client care/terms of engagement letter*]. [The expenses we have to pay to third parties will continue to be in addition to this revised price.]]

OR

[We propose to charge for the additional work by reference to the hourly rates for each fee earner involved in the matter plus VAT. The hourly rate of [*name*] is £[*amount*] and that of [*name*] is £[*amount*].]

[We estimate that the additional work involved will amount to £[*amount plus VAT*] but we shall keep you informed if the cost is likely to exceed this figure.]

Our additional charges will be added to the total of the original price of £[*amount*] which we gave to you in our letter dated [*date of client care/terms of engagement letter*].

[The expenses we have to pay to third parties will continue to be in addition to this revised estimate for our charges.]

OR

[*Specify any other charging arrangement.*]

Additional expenses

There will also be further expenses to be paid to third parties in addition to those set out in our letter dated [*date of client care/terms of engagement letter*] which amounted to £[*insert original figure for expenses itemised in letter*].

These additional likely expenses are:

£
£
£

Total   £

We anticipate that the revised total expenses to be paid to third parties will be £[*sum of amount*].

[If we find that there are yet further expenses which need to be incurred, I shall let you know the reason for the extra expense, the likely amount and when I shall need payment.]

Your continuing instructions in this matter will be taken as acceptance of our revised charges. However, we also enclose a duplicate copy of this letter and shall be grateful if you will sign and return both to us in the enclosed stamped addressed envelope as soon as possible so that we have a clear record of the revised terms of our agreement. In all other respects, these remain as set out in our letter dated [*date of client care/terms of engagement letter*] and the terms of business which accompanied that letter.

Yours sincerely

[*Signatory*]

17 Terms of business for conveyancing

The following areas are covered in these terms of business:

1. Service standards
2. Responsibilities
3. Hours of business
4. Anti-money laundering obligations
5. Speaking to your lender
6. Financial matters
7. Professional indemnity insurance
8. Equality and diversity
9. Data protection
10. Storage of papers
11. Review of files
12. Limitation of liability
13. Applicable law
14. Ending our services

1   Service standards

We aim to provide you with high standards of service at all times. We will:

- keep you regularly informed in writing of progress with your matter;
- communicate with you in plain language;
- explain to you in writing the legal work which is required as your matter progresses;
- keep you informed of the cost of your matter every month;
- keep you advised of the likely timescales for each stage of this matter and any material changes in those estimates.

2   Responsibilities

To achieve the best possible outcome in your case, we need to work together with you. We will:

- review your matter regularly;
- advise you on the law;
- follow your instructions;
- update you on whether the likely outcomes still justify the likely costs and risks associated with your matter whenever there is a material change in circumstances.

You need to:

- provide us with clear and timely instructions;
- provide us promptly with the information and documents required to complete the transaction.

3   Hours of business

Our office hours are from [*specify opening hours and working days*].

4   Anti-money laundering obligations

Evidence of identity

The law requires solicitors, banks, building societies and others to obtain satisfactory evidence of the identity of their client and, at times, people related to the client or their case. This is because solicitors who deal with money and property on behalf of their client can be used by criminals wanting to launder money.

In order to comply with the law on money laundering, we need to obtain evidence of your identity as soon as practicable, and in any event before we can proceed with your matter. To collect this evidence, our practice is to [take a photocopy of your original passport and a copy of a utility bill].

If you are unable to provide us with the specific identification requested, please contact our office as soon as possible so that we can discuss alternative ways to verify your identity.

Confidentiality

We are under a professional and legal obligation to keep details of your case confidential. This obligation, however, is subject to a statutory exception, which may require a solicitor who knows or suspects that a transaction on behalf of a client may involve money laundering or terrorist financing to make a disclosure to the Serious Organised Crime Agency.

If we are required to make a disclosure in relation to your matter, we may not be able to inform you that a disclosure has been made. We may also have to cease acting in your matter for a period of time and may not be able to tell you the reasons for it.

5   Speaking to your lender

We are also acting for your proposed lender, [*name of bank/building society*], in this transaction. This means we have a duty to make full disclosure to the mortgagee of all relevant facts relating to you, your purchase and mortgage. That will include disclosure of any discrepancies between the mortgage application and information provided to us during the transaction and any cashback payments or discount schemes which a seller is providing you. If a conflict of interest arises, we must cease to act for you in this matter.

6   Financial matters

Financial arrangements

Our practice's policy is to only accept cash up to £[*amount*] from clients.

If you try to avoid this policy by depositing cash directly with our bank, we may decide to charge you for any additional checks we decide are necessary to prove the source of the funds.

Where we have to pay money to you, it will be paid by cheque or bank transfer. It will not be paid in cash or to a third party.

Interest on money owed to you

Any money received on your behalf will be held in our practice's client account.

Subject to certain minimum amounts and periods of time set out in the Solicitors' Accounts Rules 1998, interest will be calculated and paid to you at the rate from time to time payable on [*name the bank and relevant accounts*].

The period for which interest will be paid will normally run from the date(s) on which funds are received by us, until the date(s) that cheque(s) are issued.

Costs

We have agreed a fixed fee with you in accordance with the terms of our client care letter. Expenses and VAT are payable in addition to that amount.

We will send you a bill following the exchange of contracts and payment is required before completion. If sufficient funds are available on completion, and we have sent you a bill, we will deduct our fees and expenses from the funds.

Payment of a bill is required within [*specify number*] days. We may charge you interest on unpaid bills at [*percentage*] per year, from one month after the delivery of our bill.

You are obtaining funding for this purchase from [*name of lender*]. The loan cheque must be received by us a minimum of four working days prior to the completion date. If the money can be sent by telegraphic transfer we will request that we receive it the day before completion. This will enable us to ensure that the necessary funds are available in time for completion. The lender may charge interest from the date of issue of their loan cheque or the telegraphing of the payment. For more information on these charges contact the lender directly.

Insurance advice

We are not authorised by the Financial Services Authority. We are, however, included on the register maintained by the Financial Services Authority so that we may carry on insurance mediation activity, which is broadly the advising on and selling and administration of insurance contracts. This part of our business, including arrangements for complaints or redress if something goes wrong, is regulated by the Solicitors Regulation Authority. The register can be accessed via the Financial Services Authority website at **www.fsa.gov.uk/register**.

The Law Society is a designated professional body for the purposes of the Financial Services and Markets Act 2000, but responsibility for regulation has been separated from the Law Society's representative functions. The Solicitors Regulation Authority is the independent regulatory body of the Law Society. The Legal Ombudsman deals with complaints against lawyers.

7　Professional indemnity insurance

Under the Indemnity Insurance Rules firms are required to take out and maintain qualifying insurance. Details of [*name of practice*]'s insurance can be found at our office(s), or you can contact us to request this information.

8　Equality and diversity

We are committed to promoting equality and diversity in all of our dealings with clients, third parties and employees. Please contact us if you would like a copy of our equality and diversity policy.

9　Data protection

We use the information you provide primarily for the provision of legal services to you and for related purposes including:

- updating and enhancing client records;
- analysis for management purposes and statutory returns; and
- legal and regulatory compliance.

Our use of that information is subject to your instructions, the Data Protection Act 1998 and our duty of confidentiality. Please note that our work for you may require us to disclose information to third parties such as expert witnesses and other professional advisers. You have a right of access under data protection legislation to the personal data that we hold about you.

We may from time to time send you information which we think might be of interest to you. If you do not wish to receive that information please notify our office in writing.

10 Storage of papers

We will keep our file of your papers (except any of your papers which you ask to be returned to you) for no more than six years. We will keep the file on the understanding that we have the authority to destroy it six years after the date of the final bill we send to you for this matter. We will not destroy documents you ask us to deposit in safe custody.

If we retrieve papers or documents from storage in relation to continuing or new instructions to act for you, we will not normally charge for such retrieval. However we may charge you for:

- time spent producing stored papers requested; and
- reading, correspondence or other work necessary to comply with your instructions in relation to the retrieved papers.

11 Review of files

Our practice is subject to audit or quality checks by external firms or organisations. These external firms or organisations are required to maintain confidentiality in relation to your files.

12 Limitation of liability

Our liability to you for a breach of your instructions shall be limited to £[2 million] or such other higher amount as expressly set out in the letter accompanying these terms of business. We will not be liable for any consequential, special, indirect or exemplary damages, costs or losses or any damages, costs or losses attributable to lost profits or opportunities.

These limitations apply only to the extent that they are permitted by law. In particular they do not apply to any liability for death or personal injury caused by negligence.

13 Applicable law

Any dispute or legal issue arising from our terms of business will be determined by English law and will be submitted to the exclusive jurisdiction of the English courts.

14 Ending our services

You may end your instructions to us in writing at any time, but we will be entitled to keep all your papers and documents while there is still money owing to us for charges and expenses.

We may decide to stop acting for you only with good reason. For example, if you do not pay an interim bill or there is a conflict of interest. We must give you reasonable notice that we will stop acting for you.

If you or we decide that we should stop acting for you, you will be required to pay for the expenses which we have already paid and a percentage of our fees which is considered reasonable to cover the work we have already undertaken.

18 Terms of business for litigation

> **Note:** Practices will need to determine if the Cancellation of Contracts Made in a Consumer's Home or Place of Work Regulations 2008 apply depending on the nature of the client and the circumstances in which the contract was made. Please refer to the Law Society's practice note 'Cancellation of contracts' (2010) for further guidance.

1. Service standards
2. Responsibilities
3. Hours of business
4. Anti-money laundering obligations
5. Financial matters
6. Equality and diversity
7. Professional indemnity insurance
8. Data protection
9. Storage of papers
10. Outsourcing
11. Review of files
12. Limitation of liability
13. Applicable law
14. Ending our services

1 Service standards

We aim to provide you with high standards of service at all times. We will:

- keep you informed in writing of progress with your matter each month;
- communicate with you in plain language;
- explain to you in writing the legal work which is required as your matter progresses;
- keep you informed of the cost of your matter every three months;
- keep you advised of the likely timescales for each stage of this matter and any material changes in those estimates;
- continue to review whether there are alternative methods by which your matter can be funded.

2 Responsibilities

To achieve the best possible outcome in your case, we need to work together with you. We will:

- review your matter regularly;
- advise you on the law;
- follow your instructions;
- update you on whether the likely outcomes still justify the likely costs and risks associated with your matter whenever there is a material change in circumstances.

You need to:

- provide us with clear and timely instructions;
- keep safe any documents which the court or the solicitors for [*name of opposing party*] require and provide them to us when requested.

3   Hours of business

Our office hours are from [*specify opening hours and working days*].

4   Anti-money laundering obligations

We are under a professional and legal obligation to keep your affairs confidential. This obligation, however, is subject to a statutory exception, which may require a solicitor who knows or suspects that a transaction on behalf of a client may involve money laundering or terrorist financing to make a disclosure to the Serious Organised Crime Agency.

If we are required to make a disclosure in relation to your matter, we may not be able to inform you that a disclosure has been made. We may also have to cease acting in your matter for a period of time and may not be able to tell you the reasons for it.

5   Financial matters

5.1 Financial arrangements

Our practice's policy is to only accept cash up to £[200] from clients.

If you try to avoid this policy by depositing cash directly with our bank, we may decide to charge you for any additional checks we decide are necessary to prove the source of the funds.

Where we have to pay money to you, it will be paid by cheque or bank transfer. It will not be paid in cash or to a third party.

5.2. Interest on money owed to you

Any money received on your behalf will be held in our practice's client account.

Subject to certain minimum amounts and periods of time set out in the Solicitors' Accounts Rules 1998, interest will be calculated and paid to you at the rate from time to time payable on [*name of bank and relevant accounts*].

The period for which interest will be paid will normally run from the date(s) on which funds are received by us, until the date(s) that cheque(s) are issued.

5.3 Costs

5.3.1 How we calculate charges

Our charges will be calculated by reference to the time we actually spend working on your matter. This will include:

- attending meetings and negotiations;
- reading, preparing and working on papers;
- making and responding to telephone calls, emails, faxes and letters;
- preparation of costs estimates, schedules and bills;
- attendance at court and travel time.

5.3.2 Hourly rates

Our hourly rates are set out below. We review our hourly rates each year on [*date*] to take into account increases in costs. We will notify you in writing if the rates you are being charged are increased and the date from which the increases will apply.

We will charge you £[*amount*] for each hour spent on your matter by [*name of main person responsible for the case*].

Where others are required to assist with your matter, we will charge you the following hourly rates for their work:

Grade	Description	Hourly rate
1	Partners with over 8 years' post-qualification experience	£
2	Solicitors and legal executives with over 4 years' post-qualification experience	£
3	Solicitors of less than 4 years' post-qualification experience, legal executives and fee earners of equivalent experience	£
4	Trainees, paralegals and fee earners of equivalent experience	£

All routine correspondence which we write will be charged at 1/10th of the hourly rate, while routine correspondence we receive will be charged at 1/20th of the hourly rate.

All routine telephone calls, either made or received, will be charged at 1/10th of the hourly rate.

More complicated correspondence and telephone calls will be charged at the hourly rate for the actual time they take.

If your instructions mean we have to work outside normal office hours, we may increase the level of the hourly rates. We will notify you in writing of any increases.

We will add VAT to our fees at the rate that applies when the work is completed. Currently VAT is charged at 20%.

5.3.3   Other expenses

There may be other expenses which we need to pay on your behalf. These can include:

- court fees;
- fees for expert reports;
- barristers' fees.

These will be listed separately on your bill and you may be charged VAT in relation to these expenses.

5.3.4   Payment of expenses in advance

Where we have to make payments to third parties to cover expenses such as court costs or fees for expert reports, we can ask you to pay us first. This will help prevent delays in your matter. As we become aware of payments which will need to be made we will write to you to ask you to send a cheque to us to cover the payments as the matter progresses.

When we send you bills, we will make sure we include the amounts you have already paid. If there are any advance funds left over, we will put them against our fees which need to be paid. You should note that the total bill for expenses may be greater than the amount which you have paid in advance.

5.3.5   Payment of bills

We will send you an interim bill for our fees and expenses every three months while the work is in progress. This enables you to budget as the work progresses. We will send a final bill after completion of the work.

You may also set a limit on the fees and expenses we can incur in relation to your matter. This means you have to pay our fees and expenses up to this limit, but we must ask your permission to continue working on your matter if it looks like you will have to pay us more than the limit you have set. We will write to you before we reach the limit, and explain why your matter is likely to cost more, review our estimate of how much your matter is likely to cost and ask you to agree a new limit, before we do more work on your matter.

Payment of an interim or final bill is required within [*number*] days. We may charge you interest on unpaid bills at [*percentage rate*] per year, from one month after the delivery of our bill.

If this matter does not proceed to completion, we will charge you for the work done and for expenses incurred.

We are entitled to pay your bill from monies received by us on your behalf and to retain your file papers or other property until payment is made.

5.3.6   Recovering costs

If your matter is successful, you may obtain an order from the court for the payment of your costs by another person. However, in practice this usually results in only a part of the costs being recovered for you, because of the way in which the court measures the costs.

You have to pay our charges and expenses in the first place and any amounts which can be recovered will be a contribution towards them. If the other party is in receipt of legal aid without costs entitlement or is uninsured, they simply may not be able to pay.

5.4 Other parties' costs

If you are unsuccessful in your matter, it is likely that the court will order you to pay your opponent's costs in addition to our costs. Your opponent's costs can be assessed by the court to see if they are reasonable, so you will have the opportunity to review the costs and ask the court to reduce them.

6   Equality and diversity

We are committed to promoting equality and diversity in all of our dealings with clients, third parties and employees. Please contact us if you would like a copy of our equality and diversity policy.

7   Professional indemnity insurance

Under the Indemnity Insurance Rules firms are required to take out and maintain qualifying insurance. Details of [*name of practice*]'s insurance can be found at our office(s), or you can contact us to request this information.

8   Data protection

We use the information you provide primarily for the provision of legal services to you and for related purposes including:

- updating and enhancing client records;
- analysis for management purposes and statutory returns; and
- legal and regulatory compliance.

Our use of that information is subject to your instructions, the Data Protection Act 1998 and our duty of confidentiality. Please note that our work for you may require us to disclose information to third parties such as expert witnesses and other professional advisers. You have a right of access under data protection legislation to the personal data that we hold about you.

We may from time to time send you information which we think might be of interest to you. If you do not wish to receive that information please notify our office in writing.

9   Storage of papers

After completing the work, we will be entitled to keep all your papers and documents while there is still money owing to us for charges and expenses.

We will keep our file of your papers (except any of your papers which you ask to be returned to you) for no more than six years. We will keep the file on the understanding that we have the authority to destroy it six years after the date of the final bill we send to you for this matter. We will not destroy documents you ask us to deposit in safe custody.

If we retrieve papers or documents from storage in relation to continuing or new instructions to act for you, we will not normally charge for such retrieval. However we may charge you for:

*   time spent producing stored papers requested; and
*   reading, correspondence or other work necessary to comply with your instructions in relation to the retrieved papers.

10 Outsourcing

From time to time we will outsource typing and photocopying on our files to ensure that they are dealt with in a more timely manner. We will always gain a confidentiality agreement with the outsourced service provider. Should you not want your file to be outsourced please tell us as soon as possible.

11 Review of files

Our practice is subject to audit or quality checks by external firms or organisations. These external firms or organisations are required to maintain confidentiality in relation to your files.

12 Limitation of liability

Our liability to you for a breach of your instructions shall be limited to £[2 million] or such other higher amount as expressly set out in the letter accompanying these terms of business. We will not be liable for any consequential, special, indirect or exemplary damages, costs or losses or any damages, costs or losses attributable to lost profits or opportunities.

These limitations apply only to the extent that they are permitted by law. In particular they do not apply to any liability for death or personal injury caused by negligence.

13 Applicable law

Any dispute or legal issue arising from our terms of business will be determined by English law and will be submitted to the exclusive jurisdiction of the English courts.

14 Ending our services

You may end your instructions to us in writing at any time, but we will be entitled to keep all your papers and documents while there is still money owing to us for charges and expenses.

We may decide to stop acting for you only with good reason. For example, if you do not pay an interim bill or there is a conflict of interest. We must give you reasonable notice that we will stop acting for you.

If you or we decide that we should stop acting for you, you will pay our charges up until that point on an hourly basis and expenses set out in these terms and conditions.

19 Client satisfaction survey

We aim to provide the best service to our clients. To enable us to continually improve, please give us your feedback. Answers will be kept confidential.

1.	**How satisfied were you with the overall service received from us?**

Extremely satisfied ☐   Satisfied ☐   Not satisfied ☐   Unsure ☐

Please state reasons why:

2.	**Do you think your objectives were understood?**

Yes ☐   No ☐

If no, please give reasons why:

3.	**Were you given clear advice as to your options before, during and after the matter?**

Yes ☐   No ☐

If no, please give reasons why:

3.	**Did we meet your objectives?**

Yes ☐   No ☐

If no, please give reasons why:

5.	**In general, how satisfied were you with the service you received from [*name of practice*] in relation to:**

	Extremely satisfied	Satisfied	Not satisfied	Unsure
Timeliness in responding to telephone calls, emails and letters	☐	☐	☐	☐
The turnaround time on your matter	☐	☐	☐	☐
Clarity of written communication	☐	☐	☐	☐
Quality of legal advice	☐	☐	☐	☐

6.	**Having received your bill for legal fees and costs, do you think the service we offer is value for money?**

Yes ☐   No ☐

Please give reasons why:

7.	**What could we do to improve the service you received from us?**

8.	What other services could we offer that would improve our service?

9.	Would you recommend the practice to a colleague, friend or family member?

Yes ☐   No ☐

Please give reasons why:

10.	Please use the space below for any additional comments:

Thank you for taking the time to complete this form.

Please return this form to [name] via [insert contact details].

20 File and case management checklist (Lexcel v4.1)

File no.:	
Name of organisation:	
Branch address:	
Fee earner:	
Date:	

Description of requirement		
6.13(b)	Risk profile assessment carried out and risk manager notified of unusual or high risk considerations	
6.7(b)	Key dates recorded on file and back-up system	
6.9	Conflicts of interest identified and acted upon in appropriate manner	
7.2(a)	Client's requirements and objectives communicated in writing (or as appropriate)	
7.2(b)	Clear explanation communicated to client of issues involved and options available	
7.2(c)	Explanation of what fee earner will/will not do communicated	
7.2(d)	Next steps communicated	
7.2(e)	Client informed of progress	
7.2(f)	Timescale established	
7.2(g)	Method of funding established	
7.2(h)	Merits of intended action on cost benefit analysis communicated	
7.2(i)	Appropriate level of service agreed	
7.2(j)	Responsibilities of solicitor and client explained	
7.2(k)	Name and status of person dealing with matter given	
7.2(l)	Name of person responsible for overall supervision of matter given	
7.3	Standing terms of business with regular clients recorded	
7.4(a)	Client advised of basis of charging	
7.4(b)	Client advised if charging rates to be increased	
7.4(c)	Client advised of likely payments to be made to others	

7.4(d)	Payment method discussed	
7.4(e)	Client advised of circumstances where lien for unpaid costs may be exercised	
7.4(f)	Client advised of potential liability for any other party's costs.	
6.12(c)	Record of file review retained on matter file and centrally	
6.12(d)	Corrective action identified in file review acted upon within 28 days and verified by reviewer	
6.13(c)	Change in risk profile considered and reported; risk manager informed, if appropriate	
8.2	Matter strategy/complex case project plan apparent on file	
8.3(a)	Key information recorded on file	
8.3(b)	Timely response made to telephone calls and correspondence from client/others	
8.3(c)	Continuing cost information provided	
8.3(d)	Clients informed in writing about changes of person with conduct of matter or to whom problem with service should be addressed	
8.4	Any undertakings shown clearly	
8.5(b)	Any documents, files, deeds, wills or other relevant items identifiable and traceable	
8.5(d)	Status of matter and action taken easily verified by other members of the practice	
8.5(e)	Documents stored on the matter file(s) in an orderly way	
6.14(c)	Annual risk assessment of data generated by file reviews	
8.6(b)	Client consulted in relation to selection of advocate or other professional	
8.6(c)	Client informed of name and status of expert, timescale for response and disbursements if appropriate	
7.5	Complaints handling procedure followed if any complaint raised by client	
3.3	Time spent on matter recorded on file or central system	
Procedures at end of matter (to be assessed on closed files)		
8.7(a)	Outcome and any further action required by client/practice reported to client	
8.7(b)	Client accounted to for any outstanding money	
8.7(c)	Original documents/property returned to client	
8.7(d)	Client advised about storage and retrieval of papers	
8.7(e)	Client advised whether they should review the matter in future	
6.13(e)	Concluding risk assessment undertaken by considering whether client's objectives achieved	

APPENDIX A

Lexcel v4.1 self-assessment checklist

Checklist headings

There are three headings contained in the Checklist form:

- **Mandatory requirement** – This summarises, very succinctly, what the standard requires.
- **How complied with** – This should be completed with a brief description of the relevant procedures and supporting documentation that exists within the practice.
- **Document reference** – The practice should use this column to indicate where to find relevant documentation in your practice. If individual documents are referred to, the practice should index them sequentially. For example, document A, document B, etc.

Notes

All policies and plans within the Lexcel standard require you to name the person responsible for the policy or plan, and to conduct an annual review of each policy and plan.

In relation to section 4, practices must ensure that they comply with relevant legal and regulatory provisions and staff receive appropriate training in relation to the policies.

Name of organisation:	
Assessment contact:	
Postal address:	
Telephone:	
Email:	

Mandatory requirement	How complied with	Document reference
1 **Structures and policies**		
1.1 Practices will have documentation setting out the: (a) legal framework under which they operate (b) management structure which designates the responsibilities of individuals and their accountability.		
1.2 Practices will have a risk management policy, which must include: (a) strategic risk (b) operational risk (c) regulatory risk (d) the person responsible for the policy (e) a procedure for an annual review of the policy, to verify it is in effective operation across the practice.		
1.3 Practices will have a quality policy, which must include: (a) the role the quality policy plays in the strategy of the practice (b) a process for personnel to suggest improvements to the quality system (c) the person responsible for the policy (d) a procedure for an annual review of the policy, to verify it is in effective operation across the practice.		

Mandatory requirement	How complied with	Document reference
1.4 Practices will have a policy on the avoidance of discrimination and the promotion of equality and diversity, to include: (a) employment and partnership, recruitment and selection, training and conditions of service and promotions within the practice (b) the delivery of service (c) the instruction of counsel and experts in all professional dealings (d) the person responsible for the policy (e) a procedure for an annual review of the policy, to verify it is in effective operation across the practice.		
1.5 Practices will have a policy in relation to the health and safety of all personnel and visitors to the practice, which must include: (a) the person responsible for the policy (b) a procedure for an annual review of the policy, to verify it is in effective operation across the practice.		
1.6 Practices should have a policy in relation to community and social responsibility, which must include: (a) the person responsible for the policy (b) a procedure for an annual review of the policy, to verify it is in effective operation across the practice.		
2 Strategic plans		
2.1 Practices will develop and maintain a marketing and business plan that includes measurable objectives for the next 12 months, which must include: (a) the person responsible for the plan (b) a procedure for a review of the plan to be conducted every six months to verify the plan is in effective operation across the practice.		
2.2 Practices will document the services they wish to offer, including: (a) the client groups to be served (b) how services are to be provided (c) a procedure for a review of services to be conducted every six months.		

Mandatory requirement		How complied with	Document reference
2.3	Practices will have a business continuity plan, which must include: (a) an evaluation of potential risks and the likelihood of their impact (b) ways to reduce, avoid and transfer the risks (c) key people relevant to the implementation of the plan (d) the person responsible for the plan (e) a procedure to test the plan annually, to verify that it would be effective in the event of a business interruption.		
2.4	Practices will have an information communication technology (ICT) plan, which must include: (a) the application of all ICT facilities within the practice (b) the role of ICT in facilitating services for clients (c) the person responsible for the plan (d) a procedure for an annual review of the plan, to verify it is in effective operation across the practice.		
3	**Financial management**		
3.1	Practices will document responsibility for overall financial management.		
3.2	Practices will be able to provide documentary evidence of their financial management processes, including: (a) annual budget (including, where appropriate, any capital expenditure proposed) (b) variance analysis conducted at least quarterly of income and expenditure against budgets (c) annual profit and loss or income and expenditure accounts (d) annual balance sheet (e) annual cash or funds flow forecast to be reviewed quarterly (f) quarterly variance analysis which includes at least their cash flow.		
3.3	Practices will have a time recording process which enables the accurate measurement of time spent on matters for billing purposes.		

Mandatory requirement		How complied with	Document reference
3.4	Practices will have a procedure in relation to billing clients, including:		
	(a) the frequency and terms for billing clients		
	(b) credit limits for new and existing clients		
	(c) the person responsible for the procedures		
	(d) a documented review of the procedures at least annually, to verify they are in effective operation across the practice.		
3.5	Practices will have a procedure for the handling of financial transactions, including:		
	(a) the person responsible for the procedures		
	(b) a documented review of the procedures at least annually, to verify they are in effective operation across the practice.		
4	**Information management**		
4.1	Practices will have an information management policy, which must include:		
	(a) the identification of relevant information assets of both the practice and clients		
	(b) the risk to these assets, their likelihood and their impact		
	(c) procedures for the protection and security of the information assets		
	(d) a process for training personnel		
	(e) the person responsible for the policy		
	(f) a procedure for an annual review of the policy, to verify it is in effective operation across the practice.		
4.2	Practices will have an email policy, which must include:		
	(a) the scope of permitted and prohibited use		
	(b) procedures for monitoring personnel using email		
	(c) procedures for the management and security of emails		
	(d) procedures for the storage and destruction of emails		
	(e) the person responsible for the policy		
	(f) a procedure for an annual review of the policy, to verify it is in effective operation across the practice.		

Mandatory requirement		How complied with	Document reference
4.3	If the practice has a website, the practice must have a website management policy, which must include:		
	(a) a process for document approval and publishing		
	(b) the scope of permitted and prohibited use		
	(c) procedures for the management of its security and contents		
	(d) the person responsible for the policy		
	(e) a procedure for an annual review of the policy, to verify it is in effective operation across the practice.		
4.4	If personnel in the practice have Internet access the practice must have an Internet access policy, which must include:		
	(a) the scope of permitted and prohibited use		
	(b) procedures for monitoring personnel accessing the Internet		
	(c) the person responsible for the policy		
	(d) a procedure for an annual review of the policy, to verify it is in effective operation across the practice.		
4.5	Practices will have a process for legal research, including the updating and sharing of legal and professional information.		
4.6	Practices will maintain an office manual or equivalent Intranet documentation collating information on office practice, which must be available to all personnel of the practice. This will include:		
	(a) a process to control the office manual or Intranet to ensure that only the current version is in use		
	(b) a process to update the manual or Intranet and record the date of amendments		
	(c) a central register of all policies and plans and the person responsible for them		
	(d) a procedure for an annual review of the manual, to verify it is in effective operation across the practice.		
5	People management		
5.1	Practices will have a plan for the recruitment of personnel, which must include:		
	(a) likely recruitment needs		
	(b) the person responsible for the plan		
	(c) a procedure for an annual review of the plan, to verify it is in effective operation across the practice.		

Mandatory requirement		How complied with	Document reference
5.2	Practices will have a plan for the training and development of personnel, which must include:		
	(a) the person responsible for the plan		
	(b) a procedure for an annual review of the plan, to verify it is in effective operation across the practice.		
5.3	Practices will list the tasks to be undertaken by all personnel within the practice and document the skills, knowledge and experience required for individuals to fulfil their role satisfactorily, usually in the form of a person specification.		
5.4	Practices will have procedures to deal effectively with recruitment and selection, which must include:		
	(a) the identification of vacancies		
	(b) the drafting of the job documentation		
	(c) methods of attracting candidates and applicants		
	(d) selection methods used		
	(e) storage, retention and destruction of records		
	(f) references and ID checking		
	(g) checking fee earners' disciplinary record.		
5.5	Practices will conduct an appropriate induction for all personnel, including those transferring roles within the practice and must cover:		
	(a) management structure and the individual's job responsibilities		
	(b) terms and conditions of employment		
	(c) immediate training requirements		
	(d) key policies.		
5.6	Practices will have a procedure which details the steps to be followed when a member of staff ceases to be an employee, which must include:		
	(a) the handover of work		
	(b) exit interviews		
	(c) the return of company property.		
5.7	Practices must have a training and development policy including:		
	(a) ensuring that appropriate training is provided to personnel within the practice		
	(b) ensuring that all supervisors and managers receive appropriate training		
	(c) a process to evaluate training		
	(d) the person responsible for the policy		
	(e) a procedure for an annual review of the policy, to verify it is in effective operation across the practice.		

Mandatory requirement		How complied with	Document reference
5.8	Practices will conduct a documented review of the responsibilities, objectives, performance and training of all personnel at least annually.		
6	**Supervision and operational risk management**		
6.1	Practices must designate one overall risk manager for the practice with sufficient seniority to be able to identify and deal with all risk issues which may arise.		
6.2	There will be a named supervisor for each area of work undertaken by the practice.		
6.3	Practices must have procedures to manage instructions which may be undertaken even though they have a higher risk profile, including unusual supervisory and reporting requirements or contingency planning.		
6.4	Practices must maintain lists of work that the practice will and will not undertake, including any steps to be taken when work is declined on the grounds that it falls outside acceptable risk levels. This information must be communicated to all relevant staff and must be updated when changes occur.		
6.5	Practices providing services to clients in relation to property transactions will have procedures in relation to the avoidance of involvement in mortgage fraud, including: (a) the person responsible for the procedures (b) a documented review of the procedures at least annually, to verify they are in effective operation across the practice.		
6.6	Practices must maintain details of the generic risks and causes of claims associated with the area(s) of work that is/are undertaken by the practice. This information must be communicated to all relevant staff.		
6.7	Practices must document key dates, including: (a) the definition of key dates by work type (b) key dates recorded on the file and in a back-up system.		
6.8	Practices must have a process to monitor key dates to reduce the risk of key dates being missed.		
6.9	Practices will document how they will ensure that conflicts of interest are identified and acted upon in an appropriate manner.		
6.10	Practices will have processes to ensure that all personnel, both permanent and temporary, are actively supervised. Such processes will include:		

Mandatory requirement	How complied with	Document reference
(a) checks on incoming and outgoing correspondence, including letters, emails and faxes		
(b) departmental, team and office meetings and communication structures		
(c) reviews of matter details in order to ensure good financial controls and the appropriate allocation of workloads		
(d) the exercise of devolved powers in publicly funded work		
(e) the availability of a supervisor		
(f) allocation of new work and reallocation of existing work, if necessary.		
6.11 Practices will have processes to ensure that all those doing legal work check their files regularly for inactivity.		
6.12 Practices will have a procedure for regular, independent file reviews, of either the management of the file or its substantive legal content, or both. In relation to file reviews, practices will:		
(a) define file selection criteria		
(b) define the number and frequency of reviews		
(c) retain a record of the file review on the matter file and centrally		
(d) ensure any corrective action which is identified in a file review is acted upon within 28 days and verified by the reviewer		
(e) ensure that the designated supervisor reviews and monitors the data generated by file reviews		
(f) conduct a review at least annually of the data generated by file reviews.		
6.13 Operational risk will be considered and recorded in all matters before, during and after the processing of instructions. Before the matter is undertaken the adviser must:		
(a) consider if a new client and/or matter should be accepted by the practice, in accordance with section 8.1 below		
(b) Assess the risk profile of all new instructions and notify the risk manager in accordance with procedures under 6.3 of any unusual or high risk considerations in order that appropriate action may be taken.		

Mandatory requirement	How complied with	Document reference
During the retainer the fee earner must: (c) Consider any change to the risk profile of the matter and report and advise on such circumstances without delay, informing the risk manager if appropriate (d) Inform the client in all cases where an adverse costs order is made against the practice in relation to the matter in question. At the end of the matter the fee earner must: (e) Undertake a concluding risk assessment by considering if the client's objectives have been achieved (f) Notify the risk manager of all such circumstances in accordance with documented procedures.		
6.14 Practices will analyse at least annually all risk assessment data generated within the practice. This must include: (a) any indemnity insurance claims (where applicable) (b) an analysis of client complaints trends (c) data generated by file reviews (d) the identification of remedial action.		
7 Client care		
7.1 Practices will have a policy for client care, including: (a) how enquiries from potential clients will be dealt with (b) ensuring that before taking on a client, the practice has sufficient resources and competence to deal with the matter (c) protecting client confidentiality (d) the person responsible for the policy (e) a procedure for an annual review of the policy, to verify it is in effective operation across the practice.		
7.2 Practices will communicate the following to clients in writing, unless an alternative form of communication is deemed more appropriate: (a) establish the client's requirements and objectives (b) provide a clear explanation of the issues involved and the options available to the client (c) explain what the fee earner will and will not do		

Mandatory requirement		How complied with	Document reference
	(d) agree with the client the next steps to be taken		
	(e) keep the client informed of progress, as agreed		
	(f) establish in what timescale that matter will be dealt with		
	(g) establish the method of funding		
	(h) consider whether the intended action would be merited on a cost benefit analysis		
	(i) agree an appropriate level of service		
	(j) explain your responsibilities and the client's		
	(k) the client is given the name and status of the person dealing with their matter		
	(l) the client is given the name of person responsible for the overall supervision of their matter.		
7.3	Practices must have a record of any standing terms of business with regular clients. The practice must be able to produce such terms in relation to issues covered by this section.		
7.4	Practices must give clients the best information possible about the likely overall cost of the matter, both at the outset and when appropriate, as the matter progresses, in particular practices must:		
	(a) advise the client of the basis of your charging		
	(b) advise the client if the charging rates are to be increased		
	(c) advise the client of likely payments which your practice or your client may need to make to others		
	(d) discuss with the client how they will pay		
	(e) advise the client that there are circumstances where you may be entitled to exercise a lien for unpaid costs		
	(f) advise the client of their potential liability for any other party's costs.		
7.5	Practices will operate a written complaints handling procedure, including:		
	(a) the definition of what the practice regards as a complaint		
	(b) informing the client at the outset of the matter, that in the event of a problem they are entitled to complain		
	(c) to whom the client can complain		
	(d) providing the client with a copy of your practice's complaints procedure, if requested		
	(e) once a complaint has been made, the person complaining is told in writing:		

Mandatory requirement	How complied with	Document reference
(i) how the complaint will be handled; and (ii) in what time they will be given an initial and/or substantive response (f) recording and reporting centrally all complaints received from clients (g) identifying the cause of any problems of which the client has complained offering any appropriate redress, and correcting any unsatisfactory procedures (h) the person responsible for the procedure (i) a documented review of the procedures at least annually, to verify that they are in effective operation across the practice.		
7.6 Practices will have a procedure to monitor client satisfaction across all areas of the practice.		
8 File and case management		
8.1 Practices will document how decisions will be made as to whether to accept new instructions from existing clients or instructions from clients who have not instructed the practice before.		
8.2 Practices will ensure that the strategy for a matter is always apparent on the matter file and that in complex cases a project plan is developed.		
8.3 Practices will have documented procedures to ensure that matters are progressed in an appropriate manner. In particular: (a) key information must be recorded on the file (b) a timely response is made to telephone calls and correspondence from the client and others (c) continuing cost information is provided (d) clients are informed in writing if the person with conduct of their matter changes, or there is a change of person to whom any problem with service should be addressed.		
8.4 Practices will document procedures for the giving, monitoring and discharge of undertakings.		
8.5 Practices will have a procedure to: (a) list open and closed matters, identify all matters for a single client and linked files where relevant and all files for a particular funder (b) ensure that they are able to identify and trace any documents, files, deeds, wills or any other items relating to the matter. (c) safeguard the confidentiality of matter files and all other client information (d) ensure that the status of the matter and the action taken can be easily checked by other members of the practice		

Mandatory requirement	How complied with	Document reference
(e) ensure that documents are stored on the matter file(s) in an orderly way.		
8.6 Practices will have a documented procedure for using barristers, expert witnesses and other external advisers who are involved in the delivery of legal services, which will include provision for the following:		
(a) use of clear selection criteria		
(b) where appropriate, consult with the client in relation to selection of advocate or other professional		
(c) advising the clients of the name and status of the person being instructed, how long she/he might take to respond and, where disbursements are to be paid by the client, the cost involved		
(d) maintenance of records (centrally, by department or office) on barristers and experts used, including evidence of assessment against the criteria		
(e) evaluation of performance, for the information of other members of the practice		
(f) giving clear instructions		
(g) checking of opinions and reports received to ensure they adequately provide the information sought (and, in litigation matters, comply with the rules of court and any court orders)		
(h) payment of fees.		
8.7 Practices will have documented procedures to ensure that, at the end of the matter, the practice:		
(a) reports to the client on the outcome and explains any further action that the client is required to take in the matter and what (if anything) the practice will do		
(b) accounts to the client for any outstanding money		
(c) returns to the client any original documents or other property belonging to the client if required (save for items which are by agreement to be stored by the practice)		
(d) if appropriate, advises the client about arrangements for storage and retrieval of papers and other items retained (in so far as this has not already been dealt with, for example in terms of business) and any charges to be made in this regard		
(e) advises the client whether they should review the matter in future and, if so, when and why		
(f) archives and destroys files in an appropriate manner.		

Obtaining the Law Society's *Equality and Diversity Standards and Toolkit*

Standards and toolkit

The Law Society's *Equality and Diversity Standards and Toolkit* are designed to help the legal profession to successfully promote and implement best practice in equality, diversity and inclusion – as employers, as providers of legal services, as purchasers of goods and services and in its wider role in society.

The standards and toolkit provide a road map for practices that:

- supports the six pledges of those law practices signed up to the Diversity and Inclusion Charter
- meets the requirements of the Solicitors' Code of Conduct, rule 6
- meets wider legal obligations
- helps them to better meet client expectations
- will get them in better shape to compete for business
- enables them to strive for continuous improvement
- will enhance the reputation of the profession and firms and attract and retain talented professionals.

Route to success

The Law Society and law practices understand it is vital for future business success that firms have sound tools to shape every aspect of their work. Together they have produced a 'how to' equality and diversity toolkit that will save your practice time and money.

In a challenging economy the ability to identify priorities and quickly improve performance is more important than ever. The *Equality and Diversity Standards and Toolkit* are designed to help you to deliver real results in a targeted and measured way.

Whether a sole practitioner, or a small, medium or large practice, the standards help you understand how to get started and what good and excellent look like. The publication contains an assessment tool that helps you to identify priorities. It contains videos that will help you to bring people with you and a wealth of information on what works and who can help.

Get the toolkit

If you are a senior partner or equivalent looking for help on how to lead and champion change, or a managing partner wanting to understand better the business opportunities equality and diversity can offer, or if you have training or HR responsibilities, the CD-rom has invaluable, accessible information.

The *Equality and Diversity Standards and Toolkit* are free to signatories of the Law Society's Diversity and Inclusion Charter.

For more information on the Charter go to **www.lawsociety.org.uk/inclusioncharter**.

For more information on purchasing the toolkit, email **inclusioncharter@lawsociety.org.uk**.